I VICDANSAADET SPEAKING

Abhijit Naskar is the twenty-first century Neuroscientist whose contributions in Cognitive and Behavioral Neuroscience have helped the world tackle the issues of mental illness, prejudice, hate, extremism, discrimination and segregation more effectively. As an untiring advocate of mental health and universal acceptance, he became a beloved best-selling author all over the world with his very first book "The Art of Neuroscience in Everything". With his pioneering ventures into the Neuropsychology of beliefs and biases, he has hugely contributed in the eradication of religious and cultural differences in our world, for which he is popularly hailed as the humanitarian scientist, who takes the human civilization in the path of sweet general harmony.

I VICDANSAADET
SPEAKING

No Rest Till
The World is Lifted

ABHIJIT NASKAR

I Vicdansaadet* Speaking: No Rest Till The World is Lifted

(*composed of the Turkish words 'vicdan' and 'saadet')

Copyright © 2020 Abhijit Naskar

This is a work of non-fiction

An Amazon Publishing Company, 1st Edition, 2020

Printed in the United States of America

ISBN: 9798698663225

Also by Abhijit Naskar

The Art of Neuroscience in Everything
Your Own Neuron: A Tour of Your Psychic Brain
The God Parasite: Revelation of Neuroscience
The Spirituality Engine
Love Sutra: The Neuroscientific Manual of Love
Homo: A Brief History of Consciousness
Neurosutra: The Abhijit Naskar Collection
Autobiography of God: Biopsy of A Cognitive Reality
Biopsy of Religions: Neuroanalysis towards Universal
Tolerance
Prescription: Treating India's Soul
What is Mind?
In Search of Divinity: Journey to The Kingdom of Conscience
Love, God & Neurons: Memoir of a scientist who found
himself by getting lost
The Islamophobic Civilization: Voyage of Acceptance
Neurons of Jesus: Mind of A Teacher, Spouse & Thinker
Neurons, Oxygen & Nanak
The Education Decree
Principia Humanitas
The Krishna Cancer
Rowdy Buddha: The First Sapiens
We Are All Black: A Treatise on Racism
The Bengal Tigress: A Treatise on Gender Equality
Either Civilized or Phobic: A Treatise on Homosexuality
Wise Mating: A Treatise on Monogamy
Illusion of Religion: A Treatise on Religious
Fundamentalism
The Film Testament
Human Making is Our Mission: A Treatise on Parenting
I Am The Thread: My Mission
7 Billion Gods: Humans Above All
Lord is My Sheep: Gospel of Human
Morality Absolute
A Push in Perception
Let The Poor Be Your God
Conscience over Nonsense
Saint of The Sapiens
Time to Save Medicine
Fabric of Humanity

Build Bridges not Walls: In the name of Americana
The Constitution of The United Peoples of Earth
Lives to Serve Before I Sleep
When Humans Unite: Making A World Without Borders
All For Acceptance
Monk Meets World
Mission Reality
Citizens of Peace: Beyond The Savagery of Sovereignty
Operation Justice: To Make A Society That Needs No Law
See No Gender
The Gospel of Technology
Every Generation Needs Caretakers: The Gospel of
Patriotism
Aşkanjali: The Sufi Sermon
Mad About Humans: World Maker's Almanac
Revolution Indomable
When Call The People: My World My Responsibility
No Foreigner Only Family
Hurricane Humans: Give me accountability, I'll give you
peace
Ain't Enough to Look Human
Servitude is Sanctitude
Time To End Democracy: The Meritocratic Manifesto

DEDICATION

This book is dedicated to the holiday season

CONTENTS

1. The Anti-Fanaticism Sonnet

The Anti-Fanaticism Sonnet

Acceptance begets harmony,
Reason begets solution.
Solidarity conquers agony,
Character conquers differentiation.
Humility brings sanity,
Forgiveness brings serenity.
Patience breeds tenacity,
Conscience breeds sanctity.
Observation causes insight,
Questions cause evolution.
Self-correction facilitates might,
Self-reliance facilitates ascension.
So wake up and trample all fanaticism,
Only then we'll be free from sectarianism.

2. When Calls A Promise

I made a promise to someone that I would protect humankind with my life - that I would let no savagery, no prejudice, no sectarianism tear my people apart - that I would spend every breath of my life in uniting my people - the people of earth. And my very existence is the living manifestation of that promise.

Don't make promises that you know not whether you will be able to keep, but once you do make a promise, keep it at all cost, even at the cost of your life, which is exactly the kind of promise I made - to give my life in the unification of humankind.

Initially I thought I would achieve that by erasing the religious barriers amongst people. Hence, in the beginning I wrote ceaselessly on religion, but as I kept studying the tenets of the society, I came to realize that the barriers amongst people have invaded every aspect of life and society, much beyond the mere traditional bounds of religion - they have invaded the very lifeblood of society and have been tearing the society apart from inside out.

I came to realize that the religion of the future is not going to be christianity, islam, judaism or any such traditional system, rather, the religion of the future is going to be social justice. And the best way to shape the future is to envision it early on and start manufacturing it today. Thus, though initially the primary premise of my work was religion, eventually it acquired much wider and diverse societal roots.

My purpose remains the same, that is, to unite you all, to unite my seven billion sisters and brothers of earth, but I had to make a few changes to my approach based on the need of the time as I kept evolving with my work. I started off as a scientist, but the needs of the society turned me into a reformer.

I wanted to understand human nature, but as I understood more and more - as I began to understand the nature of humanity in its true magnificence and depth - its shortfalls as well as its strongholds, and unrealized potential, I learnt about the fallacy of mere understanding. I had to put that understanding into practice, therefore, all fields of human endeavor became my work-field, with Neuroscience being the immediate ground under my feet.

Society needed not yet another scientist, it needed a reformer scientist, so I became one. All my life my need has been to serve the need of the society - need mark you, not desire. There is a difference between what the society desires and what it really needs. Society may desire for more bigotry, more segregation, more rigidity, more separatism, but that's not what the society needs - a civilized society needs humility, not bigotry - it needs inclusion, not segregation - it needs reason, not rigidity - it needs assimilation, not separatism.

3.   The Supreme Miracle

Any desire that facilitates inequality and prejudice, is nothing but savagery, whereas the need to build a just, humane and united world is the characteristic of a truly civilized and progressive society. Humanity starts with the will to build a humane society - without this will we have no right to call ourselves human. We may have plenty of pompous ideologies and schools of thought, but if we don't have an everyday concern for our society, then they are all meaningless.

It's time we change the very definition of patriotism - it's time we break our primitive loyalty to land and culture and foster a sense of servitude in its place - servitude towards the helpless - servitude towards the oppressed - servitude towards the destitute. Remember, a true healer is not the one with magical powers, but the one who does everything in their power to help those in need. Magic was an invention of ignorance, but the true magic of a civilized society lies in our capacity to help others. That's the true miracle of nature. If you help others at the fullest of your ability, then you are a miracle worker.

You don't need to memorize the bible - you don't need to turn water into wine - you don't need to have an unlimited supply of bread in your basket to be a miracle worker, you just need to have the capacity to share the one bread you have with someone hungry. If you can starve to death while sharing your bread with others, instead of appeasing your own hunger while others starve to death, that's the highest miracle of all.

Call it religion if you want - call it humanitarianism if you want - call it altruism if you want - but I call it plain ordinary humanity, without which we might as well be living in the jungle. Society means community, society means unity, society means sacrifice - if these forces run through your body like blood, then only you are a human.

Humanitarianism, altruism, holiness, all these are amateur attempts to define the basic humanity of the humans - once you learn to be a true human, all these petty terms will appear bleak and meaningless to you. When the waves of realization rise, words fade away. And only with such realization can there be true equality and assimilation in the world. Theories, philosophies, ideologies, all later, first realization. Realization is the mother of solution.

15

4. The Worth of A Human

18

If you must measure my wealth, measure it by the minds I lift, not by the money I own. Five hundred years from now, if the world is not more humane and inclusive because of me than it is today, then I would consider my life not worth a penny. The value of resources can be measured in money, but not the determination of a human.

Let me give you an example. With sheer curiosity and determination we have tamed the forces of nature to a great extent, but we are yet to tame the forces within us - we are yet to tame our own abilities. However, tame is not the right word here, that is, not when we are talking about the forces of our mind – about the forces of nature inside of us. Now comes the real question - can you place a price tag on this determination and curiosity!

And that's why no human can be measured in money. One who looks worthless today, may change the world tomorrow if they discover their stronghold. I am a living proof of it. I don't come from money nor does my family have an academic background – I didn't have wealthy friends either, yet today the whole world embraces me as a member of their own family –

and you know how it is possible – it's because never in my life I have thought of myself as little and insignificant.

This doesn't mean that I don't feel weak at times – of course I do, for being weak is a sign of life, but submitting to that weakness and letting it take over your whole being is a sign of death. So let the weakness come and go, but never give it the reigns of your life.

Walk past the weakness, discover your strongholds and put them to practice - keep working without rest till you see your dreams manifest in front of your eyes. Envision the future that you want as reality and manufacture it out of your blood and sweat. Dreams don't come true with prayers and wishes, they come true with tangible actions. Act and even the most impossible of dreams will come true. The question is not whether your dream is impossible, but whether you'll give up when things get rough.

I have a dream, that one day all humans of planet earth will stand tall with dignity and call themselves human. And this dream won't be reality in my lifetime, which is a fact that neither you nor I can ignore, but I would rather die while living for my dream than live while dying for no reason. Do you have such a dream my friend - don't compare or criticize - just look inside your heart and ask yourself, what is the reason that you exist - what is the cause in your existence - what is the movement that moves your soul! Once your heart replies back, listen to it and plunge into that movement with all that is yours.

5. Beyond Success and Failure

There is no magic to success - there is no ancestry to success - there is no status to success - there is no secret to success - there is only determination and action. However, the term success is rather shallow - it means nothing, for a human of action never stops walking, their journey continues - it continues from one goal to the next - that's what life is about - to keep walking, because the moment you stop walking, you stop living. You don't die when you stop breathing, but when you no longer have any goal in your life. Therefore, there is no success, only continued journey.

When the destination becomes more important than the journey, you no longer are pursuing a goal, but only an illusion. Remember, it's the journey that adds value to the destination, not the other around. And that's why it gives me great bliss to know for sure that I'll not reach my destination so long as I live, so I cherish every walk of my journey.

Success is a myth - a person doesn't go from failure to success - they go from one success to the next, for every failure builds your character, and any experience that builds character is an experience of success. In fact, there is no success or failure, there's only life.

Society invented terms like success and failure to judge whether a person is worthy enough to be a part of society. It's a gateway pass to an elite club filled with snobs and hypocrites, who have no idea of life, reason and progress. They are but a bunch of leeches who feed on other people's achievements while mocking the achievements that are in the making. These leeches applaud achievements and scoff at the endeavors that make those achievements possible.

Pay no heed to the sneering of these leeches, just continue with your work. It's your work that makes you who you are, not the mockery or the applause. Applause comes and goes, mockery comes and goes, it's only the work that makes you immortal. You may feel lost at times - you may be devastated at times, you may get broken at times, but gather the pieces and start walking again.

6. Partners in Progress

The strongest souls are the most broken souls. In fact, without being broken into pieces, you cannot be born as a whole human being. Those who fear brokenness, never achieve wholeness. Those who fear being lost, never find themselves. Determination delivers the path, for as I have said in my previous works, human mind is the greatest miracle of nature. Your very existence is a miracle, so either you can use that miracle to make more miracles, or you can whine about how miserable your life is. You are not going to get rid of your miseries by whining and weeping, for they'll go away on their own when you work to alleviate the miseries of others.

Light up your heart for others and their smiles will take your pain away. In the smile of others you will find your heaven. Remember, it's the servants of the people who rule the world, not the rulers. So don't try to rule, serve. Serve and you'll find serenity, serve and you'll find sanity, serve and you'll find salvation.

Footsteps of yours are the footsteps of humanity, so if you stop walking, humanity stops progressing. And this is nothing to be taken for granted. No footstep is tiny, no action is inconsequential. Change is born of the intention behind your footstep, not of the size of it.

You, me and every thinking human are partners in progress. If we throw in the towel, the world won't have any towel to cover its shameful regress. So, you must work, for the betterment of the community, for the betterment of the society, for the betterment of the world, till there is life in your veins.

Remember, without your sacrifice the dream of peace, justice and humaneness won't be fulfilled. Sacrifice all that is yours for the good of the society and the whole world will bow before you in veneration. First they'll mock you, then they'll worship you. This is the story of every legend who has done something extraordinary for the world.

And remember, recognition that comes fast, goes away fast. So, don't pay attention to the attention, pay attention to the work. People applaud the successful and mock those in the making, because by applauding the successful they feel closer to them and when they feel closer to them they feel secure, and on the other hand people mock those whose works are yet to be recognized, because they are driven by their savage subconscious to deem nonconformist dreams as a threat to their security, hence, as a threat to their survival. In short, applause and mockery are basic evolutionary behaviors of the masses. It takes a conscious practice of reason to recognize greatness in the making and shallowness in the limelight.

32

7. The Way Out of Savagery

Every move of ours in our daily life is more likely to be driven our innate savage instincts for survival than by reason and thought. This is the reason why racism, bigotry and discrimination are still dominant in our society. Till we recognize our innate savage drives and consciously override them with reason, we won't be able to eliminate primitive disharmony from our society.

Harmony and disharmony are both born of the mind, and the interesting part is, in the absence of the practice of reason and compassion, the mind automatically produces disharmony without any conscious efforts on our part, but the moment we become conscious of that disharmony and try to reason with it driven by our sense of society, the mind stops producing it.

We have only recently come out of the jungle and built civilization, that's why disharmony comes more naturally to us than harmony, and if we are to make harmony more natural than disharmony then we must make non-rigidity our way of life. And we must do so, not out of compulsion, but out of responsibility. We must do it not out of allegiance to any ideology, but out of accountability towards society - towards the world - towards the humankind.

And all of this starts with the recognition of your inner savagery, for once you begin to notice your own savagery, traditions and norms that you have held dear for so long, would automatically start to show their true face.

Perfection is an illusion that gives us comfort, hence we try to hold on to our traditions, our culture, our orthodoxy - it's all in the attempt of self-preservation. But if we are to humanize our society, we must recognize the imperfections and flaws in our nature, because only when we recognize our flaws can we take the civilized step to not be driven by those flaws, either in the name of tradition or ideology. To put it simply, there is an animal in all of us, the sooner we recognize it, the sooner we can turn human.

8. Not Left, Not Right, Only Human

It doesn't matter whether you are left or right, if you don't have the conscience and guts to recognize and eliminate the savage side of tradition and endeavor to become less animal, then you are not even worth the title human, let alone left or right. Some may say, eliminating the savage side of tradition is the very definition of leftism, and that indeed is true theoretically, but we are not talking about theories. We are talking about life - everyday, common, ordinary, wholesome life - and to taste that life, we must bring down all walls, including the walls that we build to define our theoretically progressive motives, because if a motive is truly human, then by labeling it, you only diminish its outreach and capacities.

Let no label come in the path of progress, including the labels of progressive theories and ideologies. Do whatever you do, as a human - don't let that act be defined by petty terminologies, because for every terminology that you create, somebody else will come up with a counter-terminology, and in the end, we'll all be lost in terminologies, oblivious to our universal humanity. Do what's egalitarian, do what's just, do what's non-rigid and forget the terms. Do what's humane, and let the action speak for itself.

For example, you may call me liberal, you may call me left wing, you may call me socialist - I don't have any problem with that, but I won't call myself liberal, left wing or socialist - or anything else for that matter, other than human. To put it simply, I am what a human looks like. I am not left, I am not right, I am only human. You think I am so puny that you can bottle me up with ideological wings! Ideologies may look good on pages of books, but real life requires much more than mere ideologies, it requires a genuine intention for good.

People love picking ideologies for themselves, because they try to hide their organic imperfections with the illusive perfection of ideologies. I call this perfection illusive, because the moment you bring ideology into human life, or perhaps I should say, the moment you bring human life into ideology, all the imperfections of human life become part of that ideology, even though you may choose not to recognize it, because a flawless delusion is more appealing to the human mind than a flawed reality.

9. Perfect Illusion
or Imperfect Reality

42

The human brain has not evolved to perceive reality, it has evolved to create an illusion of reality. That's why an exciting lie gains more attention than a boring truth. However, truth is anything but boring, the only reason truth appears boring to people is because they think of truth as an apple - they think all they need to do is take a bite and that would give them understanding, but in reality, truth is like an onion with infinite layers, the more layers you peel the more you understand yourself and the world. Peeling one or two layers may mean absolutely nothing but be persistent with the peeling and in time the secrets of nature would start to unfold in your mind.

Be attached to the pursuit of truth, not the truth itself, because truth is not something rigid that you can hold on to, truth is an ever-evolving force. And if your mind gets attached to the truth of today, it won't be able to accept the truth of tomorrow, and if your mind doesn't accept the evolution of truth, then it no longer walks on the path of truth, but on the path of ignorance, which only breeds more prejudice and conflicts. So, in order for there to be harmony, both inside and outside, you must accept evolution - no evolution, no progress.

For example, yesterday's truth made people religious, today's truth makes people atheist, tomorrow's truth will take people beyond both religion and atheism into the land of all-accepting humanness. Yesterday's truth made people nationalist, today's truth makes people globalist, tomorrow's truth will make people human.

Once the rigidity of religion has gone and the rebellious excitement of humanism has worn out, all that remains is an everyday, ordinary sense of humanity. Once the narrowness of nationalism has gone and the exciting newness of globalism has worn out, all that remains is an everyday, ordinary sense of humanity. And that humanity is beyond all philosophies and sophisticated ideologies, for it's the very foundation of your being. The only reason you don't feel this humanity bursting through every pore of your skin is because you are still obsessed with terms that try to imprison humanity.

Let that humanity lose and all misery will fade away from the face of this earth - how you ask - it's because once your humanity is wide awake beyond the bounds of theories and philosophies, you wouldn't be able to sit still at the sight of someone in misery. Your very humanity will make you rush to the rescue of others, just like you rush to find a glass of water when you are thirsty.

Healers don't exist, but humans do, and when you as a human lend a hand to someone in need, you turn into the highest healer there is. And no chains in the world can bind such spirit of humanity, for the spirit of humanity can't be slayed by the sword, it's the very sword that slays all inhumanity - it can't be burnt by fire, it's the fire incarnate that burns all savagery into ashes - it can't be washed away by the wind, it's the very wind that wipes out all differentiation.

The whole universe will come to your aid when your heart bleeds for others. And a heart that bleeds for others is the only human heart, all others are mere animal hearts - it is the vessel of the spirit of humanity, all others are vessels of savagery. Humanity and inhumanity are both born of the mind, so we have to make a choice out of our own free will and conscience, which one would we like to be! And remember, your choice will have irreversible repercussions in the lives of your children.

10. Humanizing Patriotism

What the world needs is patriots - but first we must revitalize the very idea of patriotism according to the needs of a civilized world - and in a civilized world mere tribal patriotism will do only harm, not good - therefore what's needed is inclusive patriotism, not a patriotism that is exclusive to the security of any one nation - what's needed is non-sectarian patriotism.

You cannot be a true patriot without respecting other nations. All nations are my own nations, but I won't force that conviction on you - however, if your respect for your own country makes you lose respect for other nations, then you are neither patriot nor human. It is this simple, if your patriotism makes you foster hate towards other nations, then it's no patriotism of a civilized society.

Let's make it simpler still. Let's forget the word patriotism for a while. And now that we don't know what that term even means, we can begin to investigate what it's supposed to mean in a civilized world. Erase all traces of the word patriotism from your psyche and saturate every pour of your mind with the word people - close your eyes, breathe in the word people - let it reach every corner of your soul - let it penetrate into the length and breadth of your entire being - fill your lungs with people, fill your heart with people, fill your veins with people - now open your eyes and look at the world - what do you see - do you see any separation - you don't, for you no longer exist as you, but every bit of your self has been saturated with an uncorrupted concern for the people - and that my friend is patriotism of a civilized world.

In a civilized world there is no my people and your people, it's all one people - it's all one existence. Each of us can grow only if we grow together as a species and not as separate entities or tribes. Disparities exist because the humans in the so-called modern society desire to grow as self-important entities - entities separate from the society. Once this selfishness vanishes, so will the disparities. And it can only start with you.

11. To Live Beyond Death

Even in death I can't rest in peace - discriminations and disparities of the world keep bringing me back to life and I'll continue to rise till assimilation becomes the first nature of humankind - who am I you ask - I am the imperishable force of oneness.

I am not talking about reincarnation mark you, for reincarnation is mere foolishness of the savage mind, what I am talking about has nothing to do with superstitious nonsense - what I am talking about is the continuation of the unifying force of humanhood across time. No death can cease the continuation of this force, for you can kill the person, but not the idea behind the person.

You can label me however you prefer, but no puny label can define my grand expanse. To do that you must find me inside your own heart. Even after studying me rigorously, if you can't perceive me as a reflection of your own soul, then you are yet to understand me. But here is the point, to understand me, that is, to understand the force of humanhood, is no work of intellect - you need much more than mere intellect to accomplish that.

Those who try to understand humanhood with mere intellect can never manifest it in their everyday life, and if you can't manifest humanhood in your everyday life, then all your investigations have gone in waste. Intellect that doesn't breed realization, is only dumbness in disguise. Realization is born of a desire for understanding. If you have such unquenchable desire, then your brain would automatically construct all the intellect that you need as you keep learning. And the beauty of it is that when you are really immersed in learning, the very term intellect turns lifeless.

12. No Belief is Beyond Scrutiny

56

When I was at university, my dorm was in a red light area. Often after class on my way to the dorm, I would sit with those sisters of mine and listen to their stories and struggles for hours - just listening to them pouring their heart out gave me a kind of uncorrupted bliss that couldn't be explained with human words. You don't need to be a practicing physician or psychiatrist to ease the pain of others, listening to them as a human being crossing prejudice is enough.

Prejudice is poison, and as such it must be thrown away as soon as it is recognized. However, the most interesting trait of prejudice is that, they do not manifest as prejudice, they simply exist in your mind as any other belief or opinion. Hence, unless you actually, on purpose scrutinize your beliefs and opinions with evidence, you won't even know that you are living a prejudiced life, and this is also the reason that prejudice exist in our world in the first place - it's because people do not like questioning their beliefs and opinions which give them a sense of comfort and security. As I said earlier, flawless delusions are more appealing to the mind than a flawed reality.

Now here some may wonder, how can accepting prejudice make our reality flawed - and the answer is, when you accept that your belief is in fact not based on any fact whatsoever, it rocks the very foundation of your personality, for our beliefs construct a great deal of our personality. It takes great character to scrutinized one's own belief, and those who can do that are the only beings worth the title human.

Once you learn to scrutinize your own beliefs, most of the separations that exist in your mind will disappear on their own. Then you'd no longer see profession, religion, status and so on, all you'll see is human. Remember, if you look at people differently because of their profession, then you are yet to be human. And when there is no longer any separation between you and others, that's when you are truly born as a human.

However, here by profession I am talking about legit professions, such as janitor, bus-driver, teacher, scientist, preacher, sex worker and so on, and not fraudulent professions, such as psychic, astrologer, empath, and so on. But, even when dealing with these frauds, you mustn't foster hate, for a great many of them are good people, even if they are deluded. So, instead of trying to break their delusion, you must work on raising your own children in a way that they won't fall prey to these frauds, and when enough conscientious humans raise their children in such a manner, soon those medieval professions will disappear due to lack of clientele.

There is no place for hate in a civilized society, no matter the excuse. Do what's needed to be done out of responsibility, not out of hate. Stand up to the conscious frauds who knowingly con people, but do so out of civilized accountability, not out of savage hate - stand up to corrupt officials and politicians who abuse their power, but do so out of civilized accountability, not out of savage hate - stand up to the wrongdoings of your fellow citizen, but do so out of civilized accountability, not out of savage hate. Hate creates chaos, accountability creates order.

13. The Anthem of
The Leader

All chaos is born of you, all order is born of you. However, here we are not talking about understanding the nature of chaos and order, for I have already done that in "Mission Reality" - here we are talking about doing our duty as humans so we could ensure everyday, ordinary order in the world outside as well as inside. And since all order of the outside world is born inside of us, we must start working on ourselves. Every generation needs a reformer, if you don't have one, be one.

There is only one anthem for the leader - for the lionhearted builder of world - sacrifice. Character of greatness is measured by sacrifice, nothing else. No pleasure, no reward, no expectation should be dear enough to overpower the desire for sacrifice in the course of societal upliftment. Either I'll lift the world or perish in the attempt - either I'll unite the world or perish in the attempt - thus speaks the torchbearer.

All change starts in the mind. Once you feel the change in your heart, only then can you bring that change into the world - only then can you lift the world. And there is no one path to lift the world - there is no one path to service. Service comes in many forms - service comes through many means. And the best way to serve the world is to use your strengths for the benefit of others.

Words come to me like equations came to Ramanujan and music came to Mozart. So I use those words to mould the very psyche of humankind in the course of a humane and inclusive future, and I do so, forgetting all pleasures of mortal life. I have only one mission in front of me - all humans will stand as one, and till they do, I won't sit still.

If music comes to you naturally, use it to move hearts - if equations come to you naturally, use them to solve the problems that haunt our society - if storytelling comes to you naturally, write stories that not only reflect the issues of our world but also provide solutions. And if you haven't found out your strength yet, then simply lend a hand to those in need.

14. Beyond Charity

The world needs sacrifice, but if you can't sacrifice all, do whatever is in your capacity. There is always something you can do for the benefit of others, and that very deed is of what the world is in need. However, here I am not talking about the so-called charity. Helping others is much more than mere charity. The greatest help you can do to a person, is to help them become self-reliant. Charity doesn't end suffering, it only postpones it. The only surefire way to end the suffering of others is to help them become self-reliant.

Here I am not referring to the sufferings of the privileged, the kind of suffering that compels them to end their life despite having everything, for most of those sufferings are self-imposed, they are born of self-centeredness - what I am talking about here is the suffering from the lack of essentials of life.

So our first concern as a civilized species must be to make sure that we build a world where no one suffers from the lack of essentials. And we cannot do that merely by giving away money. It takes much more than money to create a world free from suffering.

And the first step to free this world from suffering is to reduce our desires and empower our sense of community, for when your sense of community is wide awake, your very conscience will show you how to alleviate the suffering of your society. Of course you'll have to keep learning, but it's your own conscience that'll guide what you learn in the direction of social development.

To put it simply, you must work to distribute the fundamental resources of life equally, while working on the foundation of a society that doesn't allow disparities in distribution of resources in the first place. And to achieve that, you must break your own indifference to social disparities. Be the solution to the problem, not another critic of it. Be accountable, not judgmental.

Let me elaborate. As a scientist whose life's work has been to study human nature, one thing I've observed is that, everyone thinks they can see through others, while in reality all they really see is a reflection of their own expectations and insecurities. A humble person sees humility in everyone, whereas an arrogant person finds everyone arrogant.

Be humble, be accountable, be non-judgmental and soon the world will turn humble, accountable and non-judgmental. Discard discrimination and practice assimilation. Make every day a festival of inclusion and harmony - make every day a celebration of humanity. The human world is replete with festivals - festivals that if celebrated with a sense of humaneness, instead of a sense of cultural exclusivity, could make all discriminations powerless.

For example, thanksgiving is not just about giving thanks, it's about community and inclusion, it's about discarding prejudice and practicing humanity. Thanksgiving is not about the food, it's about the people - all people - beyond race, religion and sexuality. And the same is true for every single festival on earth. Every festival on earth belongs to every human on earth.

Festivals are occasions to empower ourselves in the course of humanity - they are the occasions to rekindle the promise of humanity in our heart - the promise that we keep forgetting in the cacophony of manmade labels.

15. Sonnet of Festivals

72

Sonnet of Festivals

Christmas isn't about the decorations,
It's about compassion.
Hanukkah isn't about the sufganiyot,
It's about amalgamation.
Ramadan isn't about the feast,
It's about affection.
Diwali isn't about the lights,
It's about ascension.
Our world is filled with festivals,
But what do they really mean?
Celebrating them with cultural exclusivity,
Makes us not human but savage fiend.
Every festival belongs to all of humanity,
For happiness has no religious identity.

74

16. To Fix The Holes in Society

Nationality has become more important than humanity - sustaining diplomacy has become more important than organizing peace. If you don't stand up to nationalist extremism now, every single nation that has been secular for a short while, such as America, Turkey, India and so on, will again turn back into the grovel-pit of bigotry, sectarianism, persecution and hate crime. And I am stating this right now, because the wheels of secularism in these nations are already starting to turn backwards.

Secularism is not an ideology, it's a fundamental characteristic of civilized humanity. In short, it's a fundamental characteristic of humanity, for without it, we ain't human, but only animal in disguise. Secularism is not left or right, it's wholeness in action. Now the question is, what is wholeness? And mark you, we no longer have the luxury to ponder upon the mystical interpretation of ancient ideas, therefore, we must bring the idea of wholeness out of the stone-age and place it in a civilized world adorning it with a civilized meaning.

Wholeness means liberty, not external liberty, but internal liberty, liberty from prejudice, liberty from discrimination, liberty from bigotry, liberty from duality or separatism. Wholeness is oneness and oneness breeds harmony. When that wholeness manifests in your mind, you'd no longer see party, religion, philosophy or ideology, all you'll see is people, and once you do, you'll be the living embodiment of secularism – you'll be the epitome of secularism.

Without being whole yourself, you can't fix the holes in the heart of society, for those holes are but reflections of incomplete humans - they are reflections of humans who only look human. To look human, to wear fancy clothes, to have university education is not what being human is about.

A hundred years of education is nothing compared to a moment spent in helping others - a hundred years wearing fancy clothes is nothing compared to a moment spent in giving the clothes off your back to someone in need. It's your behavior with others that determines whether you are human or not, not your clothes or appearance.

You may have six-pack or an hourglass figure, but that doesn't make you a human, it only makes you an appealing mating partner in the kingdom of human-looking animals, what does make you a human is being a drop of kindness amidst the sea of selfishness. Some may wonder, what can one drop of kindness do amidst the sea of selfishness! To them I say, you are a hundred oceans of kindness in a drop, all you got to do is release that force of kindness that has been in chains for ages, and soon all savage impurities of the society will be wiped out.

17. The Shape of A Human

If you want to lift the society, you must first wipe out the self. Every trace of ego is a potential poison in the course of service. And by ego I simply refer to the traces of ordinary selfishness. If you must be selfish, then be possessed by the extraordinary selfishness that makes you find pleasure in the benefit of others - that's the kind of selfishness the world needs, the selfishness that finds pleasure in instilling justice - the selfishness that finds bliss in alleviating misery - the selfishness that finds salvation in the course of assimilation.

Discard your primitive selfishness and be adorned with civilized selfishness. Remember, civilization sleeps dormant in your nerves, it must wake up - you must wake it up - how can you do that you ask - by casting it into the world through your feelings, thoughts and behavior. The only way to build a civilization is to be the civilization we want to build.

Civilization starts with us, so if we want to build a just and humane civilization, we must be just and humane ourselves. Look in the mirror - what do you see - do you see an animal that looks like a human - or do you see something more - look deeply - look beyond the shape and everything external - and you'll witness an entire civilization in the shape of a human.

The shape of a human is determined by character - no character, no human - no character, no humanity. Only when we value character over all else, can we stand as one people, and only when we stand as one people, can we instill justice and equality in the society. Sisters and brothers of planet earth, we no longer have the childish luxury to talk about toleration, for it's time to act upon assimilation, it's time for universal acceptance.

18. People Over Facts and Faith

Acceptance is simply love in practice. When you love, you accept, when you lack love, you judge. Where there is love, one bread can feed ten people, but where there is no love, even a hundred breads aren't enough for one person. Yet that's exactly the kind of world we've been raising with our utter self-centeredness. And if this continues all the resources in the world won't be able to save our species from the imminent doom that's gaining on us.

Remember, if we don't learn to break bread with each other, there'll come a day when none of us will have any bread to break. There's suffering in the world, not because there is lack of resources but because those resources are not distributed equally, and it is so, because of our own selfishness, because of our own savagery.

In a civilized society, assimilation should be the supreme principle, not divisiveness, yet the reality is, we live in a world where not only divisiveness is the principle, but on top of that, we justify that divisiveness with all sorts of ideological nonsense, and to defend those nonsense we come up with more ideologies.

Acceptance and reason can no longer remain as mere bookish theories, they must become the way of life for every living human on earth. And when I say living human, I mean those humans who have the capacity to feel and think, not those who'd rather obstinately cling to tradition and destroy the world in the process, instead of waking up to the needs of the new age. Traditions are part of life, but they must evolve with time, if they don't, they become poison.

Don't foster that poison in your heart o brave titan, be an ever-evolving force of nature and adapt your feelings, thoughts and actions according to the needs of the time. But mind you, I am not talking about an utter, cold obsession over facts - obsession over facts is as dangerous as blind faith. Let me elaborate.

People often ask me, *"you are not a believer in the common sense of the term, then why don't you call yourself an atheist"*, I tell them, *"that's because atheists place all importance on facts, I place all importance on people"*. As a scientist, I am very much aware of the value of facts, but facts are never more important than the people, in fact, they are only valuable so long as they serve the welfare of people - in circumstances where facts go against the welfare of the people, a civilized human must always choose people over facts.

Therefore, to the militant atheist I say, there's more to life than cold facts. And at the same time, to the religious fanatics I say, there's more to life than blind faith. To put it simply, there's more to life than blind faith and cold facts. What are you going to do with all the facts, if there is no people around - and what are you going to do with all the scriptures if there is no people around! Whether there is a supreme almighty, is no concern of mine, all I care about is the upliftment of the humans by the humans - by me, you and by every single creature who calls themselves human.

Of course, we must make reason an essential part of everyday life, but we cannot do that simply by forcing facts on people. Being illogical is not the problem, for a purely logical world is as lifeless as a purely illogical one. We must distinguish the harmful illogicalities from the acceptable ones, and work towards eliminating them from the society, not merely with facts presented raw, but with facts immersed in a whole lot of love.

19. The Anti-Stereotype Sonnet

The Anti-Stereotype Sonnet

Black is not evil.
White is not trash.
Brown is not illegal.
Muslims don't crash.
Women ain't weak.
Jews ain't greedy.
Men ain't playboys.
Queer ain't sickly.
Hijab is not oppression.
Hourglass ain't beauty.
Faith is not delusion.
Atheists don't lack morality.
Assumptions only reveal shallowness.
Beyond stereotypes lies humaneness.

20. Beyond The Narrative

Being righteous and being right are two different things, one indicates morality, another indicates rationality, and we need a healthy balance between both to live and prosper with health, sanity and serenity. We mustn't go back to living in caves by compromising all rationality, but at the same time, we mustn't practice rationality to such an extreme that we kill the very warmth of the human spirit.

The point is, humans are not machines that can live on logic alone, we need emotions, we need sentiments, we need warmth, all of which are beyond the capacity of logic. This doesn't mean logic is completely expendable. What this means is that we must develop the mental faculty to recognize when to let emotions win and logic lose and vise-versa.

Let me elaborate. If you are run by emotions alone, any institution with the intention and resources to manipulate the thinking of the masses, such as the media or the state, can manipulate your thoughts and behavior through your emotions quite easily, like they are doing right now in Azerbaijan and India.

When the people don't give a damn about reason, they can be manipulated quite easily - and in such cases the perception of the people are manufactured by those controlling the narratives. As a result, ask an Azerbaijani, *"who do you think is at fault for the conflict at Nagorno-Karabakh"* and they'll say, *"Armenia of course"* - or ask an Indian, *"who do you think is at fault for the conflict at Jammu-Kashmir"*, they'll say, *"Pakistan of course"*.

Hard as it may sound, whoever controls the narrative, controls the people. This means that the very lives of the people are controlled by those who control the narrative. And the only way to break that spell is to practice reason, but without losing your warmth. Warmth without reason leads to regress, reason without warmth leads to lifelessness.

21. When Warmth and Reason Combine

The purpose of reason is not to turn this world cold, but to rid it of biases - of prejudice. Our life in the wild filled us with prejudice, but nature gave us the antidote to that prejudice as well, it's reason. Reason is the only cure for prejudice, for when the mind is filled with biases, even sentiments work in favor of those biases - the only way out is by means of reason.

Now the question is, why do we need to practice reason - and the answer is, we need to practice reason so that we could become less animal and more human - we need to practice reason so that we can make way for warmth and we need to practice warmth so that we can make way for reason. Reason and warmth must work as one force of humanity, not as separate constructs of the self-obsessed psyche.

When human reason and human warmth become one, self and society are bound to become one. And when they do, the very terms humanitarianism, altruism, holiness will exist only on the pages of history books - for every human will be a humanitarian, every human will be an altruist, every human will be holiness incarnate.

BIBLIOGRAPHY

Archer M., (2000), Being Human: The Problem of Agency. Cambridge University Press.

Archer M., (2003), Structure, Agency and the Internal Conversation. Cambridge University Press.

Adolphs R (2003) Cognitive neuroscience of human social behaviour. Nature Rev Neurosci 4: 165–178.

Adolphs R, Tranel D, Damasio AR (2003) Dissociable neural systems for recognizing emotions. Brain Cogn 52: 61–69.

Afton, A. D. (1985). Forced copulation as a reproductive strategy of male lesser scaup: A field test of some predictions. - Behaviour 92, p. 146-167.

Allison T, Puce A, McCarthy G. (2000) Social perception from visual cues: role of the STS region. Trends Cogn Sci 4: 267–278.

Andresen, Jensine, and Robert Forman, eds. Cognitive Models and Spiritual Maps. Bowling Green, Ohio: Imprint Academic, 2000.

Ashbrook, James, and Carol Albright. The Humanizing Brain: Where Religion and Neuroscience Meet. Cleveland, OH: Pilgrim Press, 1997.

Azari, Nina, Janpeter Nickel, Gilbert Wunderlich, Michael Niedeggen, Harald Hefter, Lutz Tellmann, Hans Herzog, Petra Stoerig, Dieter Birnbacher, and Rudiger Seitz. "Neural Correlates of Religious Experience." European Journal of Neuroscience 13, no. 8 (2001)

Agar, N. (2004). Liberal eugenics: In defence of human enhancement. London: Blackwell Publishing.

Alteheld, N., Roessler, G., Vobig, M., & Walter, R. (2004). The retina implant new approach to a visual prosthesis. Biomedizinische Technik, 49(4), 99–103.

Antal, A., Nitsche, M. A., Kincses, T. Z., Kruse, W., Hoffmann, K. P., & Paulus, W. (2004a). Facilitation of visuo-motor learning by transcranial direct current stimulation of the motor and extrastriate visual areas in humans. European Journal of Neuroscience, 19(10), 2888–2892.

Bhat Z, Kumar, S, Bhat H (2015) In vitro meat production. Challenges and benefits over conventional meat production. J Sci Food Agric 14: 241–248

Bernstein R. J., (1967), John Dewey. New York: Washington Square Press.

Bernstein R.J., (1971), Praxis and Action: Contemporary Philosophies of Human Activity. Philadelphia: University of Pennsylvania Press.

Bernstein R.J., (1976), The Restructuring Social and Political Thought.

Bernstein R.J., (1983), Beyond Relativism and Objectivism: Science, Hermeneutics, and Praxis. Philadelphia: University of Pennsylvania Press.

Bernstein R.J., (1986), Philosophical Profiles. Philadelphia: University of Pennsylvania Press.

Bernstein R.J., (1991), New Constellation. Cambridge: MIT Press.

Barash, D. P. (1977). Sociobiology of rape in mallards (Anas platyrhynchos): Responses of the mated male. - Science 197, p. 788-789.

Berger, J. (1986). Wild horses of the great basin: Social competition and population size. - The University of Chicago Press, Chicago.

Birkhead, T. R., Johnson, S. D. & Nettleship, D. N. (1985). Extra-pair matings and mate guarding in the common murre Uria aalge. - Anim. Behav. 33, p. 608-619.

Beauregard, Mario, and Vincent Paquette. "Neural Correlates of a Mystical Experience in Carmelite Nuns." Neuroscience Letters 405, no. 3 (2006)

Benson, Herbert. Timeless Healing: The Power and Biology of Belief. New York: Scribner, 1996

Bogen, J.E.(1995a), 'On the neurophysiology of consciousness: Part I. An overview', Consciousness and Cognition, 4.

Bogen, J.E. (1995b), 'On the neurophysiology of consciousness: Part II. Constraining the semantic problem', Consciousness and Cognition, 4.

Bremner, J. D., R. Soufer, et al. (2001). "Gender differences in cognitive and neural correlates of remembrance of emotional words." Psychopharmacol Bull 35 (3).

Brothers, L. (2002). The social brain: A project for integrating primate behavior and neurophysiology in a new domain. In J. T. Cacioppo et al. (Eds.), Foundations in neuroscience. Cambridge, MA: MIT Press.

Buss, D. D. (2003). Evolutionary Psychology: The New Science of Mind, 2nd ed. New York: Allyn & Bacon.

Buss, D. M. (1989). "Conflict between the sexes: Strategic interference and the evocation of anger and upset." J Pers Soc Psychol 56 (5).

Buss, D. M. (1995). "Psychological sex differences. Origins through sexual selection." Am Psychol 50 (3).

Buss, D. M. (2002). "Review: Human Mate Guarding." Neuro Endocrinol Lett 23 (Suppl 4).

Buss, D. M., and D. P. Schmitt (1993). "Sexual strategies theory: An evolutionary perspective on human mating." Psychol Rev 100 (2).

Blakemore SJ, Decety J (2001) From the perception of action to the understanding of intention. Nature Rev Neurosci 2: 561.

Bruce C, Desimone R, Gross CG (1981) Visual properties of neurons in a polysensory area in superior temporal sulcus of the macaque. J Neurophysiol 46: 369–384.

Buccino G, Vogt S, Ritzl A, Fink GR, Zilles K, Freund HJ, Rizzolatti G (2004) Neural circuits underlying imitation of hand actions: an event related fMRI study. Neuron 42: 323–34.

Colapietro V., (1988), "Human Agency: The Habits of Our Being."

Southern Journal of Philosophy, XXVI, 2, pp. 153-68.

Colapietro V., (1992), "Purpose, Power, and Agency." The Monist, 75, 4 (October) pp. 423-44.

Colapietro V., (2003), "Signs and their vicissitudes: Meanings in excess of consciousness and functionality." Logica, Dialogica, Ideologica, a cure di Susan Petrilli e Patrizia Calefato (Milano: Mimesis), pp. 221-36.

Colapietro V., (2004a), "C. S. Peirce's Reclamation of Teleology." Nature in American Philosophy, ed. Jean De Groot (Washington, D.C.: Catholic University Press of America), pp. 88-108.

Colapietro V., (2004b), "Portrait of a Historicist: An Alternative Reading of Peircean Semiotic." Semiotiche, 2/04 [maggio 2004], pp. 49-68.

Colapietro V., (2006), "Engaged Pluralism: Between Alterity and

Sociality." The Pragmatic Century: Conversations with Richard J. Bernstein (Albany, NY: SUNY Press), pp. 39-68.

Colapietro V., (2009), "Habit, Competence, and Purpose." Forthcoming in The Transactions of the Charles S. Peirce Society. Calder AJ, Keane J, Manes F, Antoun N, Young AW (2000) Impaired recognition and experience of disgust following brain injury. Nature Neurosci 3: 1077–1078.

Carey DP, Perrett DI, Oram MW (1997) Recognizing, understanding and reproducing actions. In: Jeannerod M, Grafman J (eds) Handbook of neuropsychology. Vol. 11: Action and cognition. Elsevier, Amsterdam.

Carr L, Iacoboni M, Dubeau MC, Mazziotta JC, Lenzi GL (2003) Neural mechanisms of empathy in humans: a relay from neural systems for imitation to limbic areas. Proc Natl Acad Sci USA 100: 5497–5502.

Changeux JP, Ricoeur P (1998) La nature et la règle. Odile Jacob, Paris.

Cochin S, Barthelemy C, Roux S, Martineau J (1999) Observation and execution of movement: similarities demonstrated by quantified electroencephalograpy. Eur J Neurosci 11: 1839– 1842.

Chomsky Noam, (2017) Requiem for the American Dream

Chomsky Noam, (2016) Who Rules the World?

Chomsky Noam, (2010) How the World Works

Churchland, P.S. (1986), Neurophilosophy (Cambridge, MA: The MIT Press).

Churchland, P.S. & Ramachandran, V.S. (1993), 'Filling in: Why Dennett is wrong', in Dennett and His Critics:

Demystifying Mind, ed. B. Dahlbom (Oxford: Blackwell Scientific Press).

Churchland, P.S., Ramachandran, V.S. & Sejnowski, T.J. (1994), 'A critique of pure vision', in Large- scale Neuronal Theories of the Brain, ed. C. Koch & J.L. Davis (Cambridge, MA: The MIT Press).

Crick, F. (1994), The Astonishing Hypothesis: The Scientific Search for the Soul (New York: Simon and Schuster).

Crick, F. (1996), 'Visual perception: rivalry and consciousness', Nature, 379.

Crick, F. & Koch, C. (1992), 'The problem of consciousness', Scientific American, 267.

Craig AD (2002) How do you feel? Interoception: the sense of the physiological condition of the body. Nature Rev Neurosci 3: 655–666.

Damasio, A (2003a) Looking for Spinoza. Harcourt Inc. Damasio A (2003b) Feeling of emotion and the self. Ann NY Acad Sci 1001: 253–261.

d'Aquili, Eugene. "Senses of Reality in Science and Religion." Zygon 17, no 4 (1982)

d'Aquili, Eugene. "The Biopsychological Determinants of Religious Ritual Behavior." Zygon 10, no. 1 (1975)

d'Aquili, Eugene. "The Myth-Ritual Complex: A Biogenetic Structural Analysis." Zygon 18, no. 3 (1983)

d'Aquili, Eugene, and Andrew Newberg. The Mystical Mind: Probing the Biology of Religious Experience. Minneapolis: Fortress Press, 1999.

Daly DD. 1958. Ictal affect. Am J Psychiatry.

Damasio, A. (1994) Descartes' Error: Emotion, Reason and the Human Brain. New York, Putnams.

Damasio, A. (1999) The Feeling of What Happens: Body, Emotion and the Making of Consciousness. London, Heinemann.

Darwin, C. (1859) On the Origin of Species by Means of Natural Selection. London, Murray.

Darwin, C. (1871) The Descent of Man and Selection in Relation to Sex. London, John Murray.

Darwin, C. (1872) The Expression of the Emotions in Man and Animals. London, John Murray; also published 1965, Chicago, University of Chicago Press.

Dawkins, M.S. (1987) Minding and mattering. In C. Blakemore and S. Greenfield (eds) Mindwaves. Oxford, Blackwell, 151-60.

Dawkins, R. (1976) The Selfish Gene. Oxford, Oxford University Press; a new edition, with additional material, was published in 1989.

Dawkins, R. (1986) The Blind Watchmaker. London, Longman.

Di Pellegrino G, Fadiga L, Fogassi L, Gallese V, Rizzolatti G (1992) Understanding motor events: A neurophysiological study. Exp Brain Res 91: 176–80.

Deikman, A.J. (2000) A functional approach to mysticism. Journal of Consciousness Studies 7(11-12), 75-91.

Delmonte, M.M. (1987) Personality and meditation. In M. West (ed.) The Psychology of Meditation. Oxford, Clarendon Press, 118-32.

Dennett, D.C. (1987) The Intentional Stance. Cambridge, MA, MIT Press.

Dennett, D.C. (1988) Quining qualia. In A.J. Marcel and E. Bisiach (eds)

Consciousness in Contemporary Science. Oxford, Oxford University Press, 42-77.

Dennett, D.C. (1991) Consciousness Explained. Boston, MA, and London, Little, Brown and Co.

Dennett, D.C. (1995a) Darwin's Dangerous Idea. London, Penguin.

Dennett, D.C. (1995b) The unimagined preposterousness of zombies. Journal of Consciousness Studies 2(4), 322-6.

Dennett, D.C. (1995c) Cog: steps towards consciousness in robots. In T. Metzinger (ed.) Conscious Experience. Thorverton, Devon, Imprint Academic, 471-87.

Dennett, D.C. (1995d) The path not taken. Behavioral and Brain Sciences 18, 252-3; commentary on N. Block, On a confusion about a function of consciousness. Behavioral and Brain Sciences 18, 227.

Dennett, D.C. (1996a) Facing backwards on the problem of consciousness. Journal of Consciousness Studies 3(1), 4-6.

Dennett, D.C. (1996b) Kinds of Minds: Towards an Understanding of Consciousness. London, Weidenfeld & Nicolson.

Dennett, D.C. (1997) An exchange with Daniel Dennett. In J. Searle (ed.) The Mystery of Consciousness. New York, New York Review of Books, 115-19.

Dennett, D.C. (1998) The myth of double transduction. In S.R. Hameroff, A.W. Kaszniak and A. C. Scott (eds) Toward a Science of Consciousness: The Second Tucson Discussions and Debates. Cambridge, MA, MIT Press, 97-107.

Dennett, D.C. (1998b) Brainchildren: Essays on Designing Minds. Cambridge, MA, MIT Press.

Dennett, D.C. (2001) The fantasy of first person science. Debate with D. Chalmers, Northwestern University, Evanston, IL, February 2001.

Dennett, D.C. (2003) Freedom Evolves. New York, Penguin.

Dennett, D.C. and Kinsbourne, M. (1992) Time and the observer: the where and when of consciousness in the brain. Behavioral and Brain Sciences 15, 183-247, including commentaries and authors' responses.

Dewey J., (1911 [1977]), "Epistemological Realism: The Alleged Ubiquity of the Knowledge Relation." Journal of Philosophy, VIII, 20 (September 28, 1911).

Dewhurst, Kenneth, and A. W. Beard. "Sudden Religious Conversions in Temporal Lobe Epilepsy." British Journal of Psychiatry 117 (1970)

Dewhurst K, Beard AW. Sudden religious conversions in temporal lobe epilepsy. 1970 Epilepsy Behav 2003

Devinsky O, Lai G. Spirituality and religion in epilepsy. Epilepsy Behav 2008.

Devinsky, O., Morrell, MJ, Vogt, BA. (1995) 'Contribution of anterior cingulate cortex to behavior', Brain, 118.

Douglas Stone A., Chapter 24, The Indian Comet, in the book Einstein and the Quantum, Princeton University Press, Princeton, New Jersey, 2013.

E. Horvitz, "One Hundred Year Study on Artificial Intelligence: Reflections and Framing," ed: Stanford University, 2014.

Einstein A. (1925). "Quantentheorie des einatomigen idealen Gases". Sitzungsberichte der Preussischen Akademie der Wissenschaften.

Eckhart Meister, Selected Writings

Egidi R., ed. (1999), "Von Wright and 'Dante's Dream': Stages in a Philosophical Pilgrim's Progress", in In Search of a New Humanism: the Philosophy of G.H. von Wright, ed. by R. Egidi, Kluwer, Dordrecht.

Fadiga L, Fogassi L, Pavesi G, Rizzolatti G (1995) Motor facilitation during action observation: a magnetic stimulation study. J Neurophysiol 73: 2608–2611.

Fogassi L, Gallese V, Fadiga L, Rizzolatti G (1998) Neurons responding to the sight of goal directed hand/arm actions in the parietal area PF (7b) of the macaque monkey. Soc Neurosci Abs 24:257.5.

Frith U, Frith CD (2003) Development and neurophysiology of mentalizing. Philos Trans R Soc Lond B Biol Sci 358: 459.

Farah, M.J. (1989), 'The neural basis of mental imagery', Trends in Neurosciences, 10.

Finlay BL, Darlington RB (1995) Linked regularities in the development and evolution of mammalian brains. Science 268.

Freud, S. "The Interpretation of Dreams", 1900

Freud, S. "Selected papers on hysteria and other psychoneuroses" Journal of Nervous and Mental Disease 1909.

Freud, S. "The Origin and Development of Psychoanalysis", 1910

Freud, S. "Psychopathology of everyday life", 1914

Freud, S. "Beyond the Pleasure Principle", 1920

Frith, C.D. & Dolan, R.J. (1997), 'Abnormal beliefs: Delusions and memory', Paper presented at the May,

1997, Harvard Conference on Memory and Belief.

Gay, Volney, ed. Neuroscience and Religion. Plymouth, UK: Lexington Books, 2009.

Gazzaniga, M. S. (1985). The social brain. New York: Basic Books.

Gazzaniga, M.S. (1993), 'Brain mechanisms and conscious experience', Ciba Foundation Symposium, 174.

Geschwind N. "Behavioural changes in temporal lobe epilepsy". Psychol Med. 1979.

Gellhorn, E., Kiely, W.F. "Mystical states of consciousness: neurophysiological and clinical aspects." J Nerv Ment Dis. 1972;154:399-405.

Gilbert SL, Dobyns WB, Lahn BT (2005) Genetic links between brain development and brain evolution. Nat Rev Genet 6.

Gray JA. The Psychology of Fear and Stress. 2nd ed. New York, NY: Cambridge University Press; 1988.

Gloor, P. (1992), 'Amygdala and temporal lobe epilepsy', in The Amygdala: Neurobiological Aspects of Emotion, Memory and Mental Dysfunction, ed J.P. Aggleton (New York: Wiley-Liss).

Greenspan, S. I. and S. G. Shanker (2004). The first idea: How symbols, language, and intelligence evolved from our early primate ancestors to modern humans. Cambridge, MA: Da Capo Press.

Grady, D. (1993), 'The vision thing: Mainly in the brain', Discover, June.

Gallagher HL, Frith CD (2003) Functional imaging of 'theory of mind'. Trends Cogn Sci 7: 77.

Gallese V, Fogassi L, Fadiga L, Rizzolatti G (2002) Action representation and the inferior parietal lobule. In: Prinz W, Hommel B (eds) Attention & Performance XIX. Common mechanisms in perception and action. Oxford University Press, Oxford.

Gallese V, Keysers C, Rizzolatti G (2004) A unifying view of the basis of social cognition. Trends Cogn Sci 8: 396–403.

Gangitano M, Mottaghy FM, Pascual-Leone A (2001) Phase specific modulation of cortical motor output during movement observation. NeuroReport 12: 1489–1492.

Gangitano M, Mottaghy FM, Pascual-Leone A (2004) Modulation of premotor mirror neuron activity during observation of unpredictable grasping movements. Eur J Neurosci 20: 2193– 2202.

Goldman AI, Sripada CS (2004) Simulationist models of face-based emotion recognition. Cognition 94: 193–213.

Grèzes J, Costes N, Decety J (1998) Top-down effect of strategy on the perception of human biological motion: a PET investigation. Cogn Neuropsychol 15: 553–582.

Grèzes J, Armony JL, Rowe J, Passingham RE (2003) Activations related to "mirror" and "canonical" neurones in the human brain: an fMRI study. Neuroimage 18: 928–937.

Gross CG, Rocha-Miranda CE, Bender DB (1972) Visual properties of neurons in the inferotemporal cortex of the macaque. J Neurophysiol 35: 96–111.

Hari R, Forss N, Avikainen S, Kirveskari S, Salenius S, Rizzolatti G (1998) Activation of human primary motor cortex during action observation: a neuromagnetic study.

Proc. Natl Acad Sci USA 95: 15061–15065.

Hardy, G. H. (1940). Ramanujan. Cambridge: Cambridge University Press.

Hall, Daniel, Keith Meador, and Harold Koenig. "Measuring Religiousness in Health Research: Review and Critique." Journal of Religion and Health 47, no. 2 (2008)

Harris, Sam, Jonas Kaplan, Ashley Curiel, Susan Bookheimer, Marco Iacoboni, and Mark Cohen. "The Neural Correlates of Religious and Nonreligious Belief." PLoS One 4, no. 10 (October 1, 2009)

Halgren, E. (1992), 'Emotional neurophysiology of the amygdala within the context of human cognition', in The Amygdala: Neurobiological Aspects of Emotion, Memory and Mental Dysfunction, ed J.P. Aggleton (New York: Wiley-Liss).

Halligan PW, Fink GR, Marshal JC, Vallar G. 2003. Spatial cognition: evidence from visual neglect. Trends Cogn Sci.

Handbook of Emotions, Edited by Michael Lewis, Jeannette M. Haviland-Jones, and Lisa Feldman Barrett, The Guilford Press; 3rd edition (2010).

Haggard, P., Clark, S. and Kalogeras,]. (2002) Voluntary action and conscious awareness, Nature Neuroscience 5, 382-5. Haggard, P., Newman, C. and Magno, E. (1999) On the perceived time of voluntary actions. British Journal of Psychology 90, 291-303.

Hameroff, S.R. and Penrose, R. (1996) Conscious events as orchestrated space-time selections. Journal of Consciousness Studies 3(1), 36-53; also reprinted in J. Shear (ed.) (1997) Explaining Consciousness-The Hard Problem. Cambridge, MA, MIT Press, 177-95.

Hardcastle, V.G. (2000) How to understand theN in NCC. InT. Metzinger (ed.) Neural Correlates of Consciousness. Cambridge, MA, MIT Press, 259-64.

Harding, D.E. (1961) On Having no Head: Zen and the Re-Discovery of the Obvious. London, Buddhist Society.

Hardy, A. (1979) The Spiritual Nature of Man: A Study of Contemporary Religious Experience. Oxford, Clarendon Press.

Hamad, S. (1990) The symbol grounding problem. Physica D 42, 335-46.

Hamad, S. (2001) No easy way out. The Sciences 41(2), 36-42.

Harre, R. and Gillett, G. (1994) The Discursive Mind. Thousand Oaks, CA, Sage.

Haugeland, J. (ed.) (1997) Mind Design II: Philosophy, Psychology, Artificial

Intelligence. Cambridge, MA, MIT Press.

Hauser, M.D. (2000) Wild Minds: What Animals Really Think. New York, Henry Holt and Co.; London, Penguin.

Hearne, K. (1990) The Dream Machine. Northants, Aquarian.

Hebb, D.O. (1949) The Organization of Behavior. New York, Wiley.

Helmholtz, H.L.F. von (1856-67) Treatise on Physiological Optics.

Hess, EH (1975) "The role of pupil size in communication," Scientific American, 233(5), 110–12.

Heyes, C.M. (1998) Theory of mind in nonhuman primates. Behavioral and Brain Sciences 21, 101-48; with commentaries.

Heyes, C.M. and Galef, B.G. (eds) (1996) Social Learning in Animals: The Roots of Culture. San Diego, CA, Academic Press.

Hilgard, E.R. (1986) Divided Consciousness: Multiple Controls in Human Thought and Action. New York, Wiley.

Hocquette JF (2016) Is in vitro meat the

solution for the future? Meat Science 120:

167–176

Hodgson, R. (1891) A case of double consciousness. Proceedings of the Society for Psychical Research 7, 221-58.

Hofstadter, D.R. (1979) Code!, Escher, Bach: An Eternal Golden Braid. London, Penguin.

Hofstadter, D.R. and Dennett, D.C. (eds) (1981) The Mind's I: Fantasies and Reflections on Self and Soul. London, Penguin.

Holland, J. (ed.) (2001) Ecstasy: The Complete Guide: A Comprehensive Look at the Risks and Benefits of

MDMA. Rochester, VT, Park Street Press.

Holmes, D.S. (1987) The influence of meditation versus rest on physiological arousal. In M. West (ed.) The Psychology of Meditation. Oxford, Clarendon Press, 81-103.

Holt, J. (1999) Blindsight in debates about qualia. Journal of Consciousness Studies 6(5), 54-71.

Horgan, J. (1994), 'Can science explain consciousness?', Scientific American, 271.

Holloway RL (1996) Evolution of the human brain. In: Lock A, Peters CR (eds) Handbook of human symbolic evolution. Oxford University Press, Oxford

Iacoboni M, Woods RP, Brass M, Bekkering H, Mazziotta JC, Rizzolatti G (1999) Cortical mechanisms of human imitation. Science 286: 2526–2528.

Iacoboni M, Koski LM, Brass M, Bekkering H, Woods RP, Dubeau MC, Mazziotta JC, Rizzolatti G (2001) Reafferent copies of imitated actions in the right superior temporal cortex. Proc Natl Acad Sci USA 98: 13995–13999.

Jeannerod M (1988) The neural and behavioural organization of goal-directed movements. Clarendon Press, Oxford.

Johnson-Frey SH, Maloof FR, Newman-Norlund R, Farrer C, Inati S, Grafton ST (2003) Actions or hand-objects interactions? Human inferior frontal cortex and action observation. Neuron 39: 1053–1058.

Jackson, F. (1982) Epiphenomenal qualia. Philosophical Quarterly 32, 127-36.

James, W. (1890) The Principles of Psychology (2 volumes). London, Macmillan.

James, W. (1902) The Varieties of Religious Experience: A Study in Human Nature. New York and London, Longmans, Green and Co.

Jansen, K. (2001) Ketamine: Dreams and Realities. Sarasota, FL, Multidisciplinary Association for Psychedelic Studies.

Jay, M. (ed.) (1999) Artificial Paradises: A Drugs Reader. London, Penguin.

Jaynes, J. (1976) The Origin of Consciousness in the Breakdown of the Bicameral Mind. New York, Houghton Mifflin.

Johnson, M.K. and Raye, C.L. (1981) Reality monitoring. Psychological Review 88, 67-85.

Kadim I, Mahgoub O, Baqir S et al. (2015) Cultured meat from muscle stem cells: a review of challenges and prospects. J Integr Agr 14: 222–233

Koski L, Iacoboni M, Dubeau MC, Woods RP, Mazziotta JC (2003) Modulation of cortical activity during different imitative behaviors. J Neurophysiol 89: 460–471.

Krolak-Salmon P, Henaff MA, Isnard J, Tallon-Baudry C, Guenot M, Vighetto A, Bertrand O, Mauguiere F (2003) An attention modulated response to disgust in human ventral anterior insula. Ann Neurol 53: 446–453.

Kandel, E. R. In Search of Memory: The Emergence of a New Science of Mind, W. W. Norton & Company (2007).

Kandel E. R. Schwartz JH, Jessel TM. Principles of neural sciences. New York; McGraw Hill, 2000.

Kanizsa, G. (1979), Organization In Vision (New York: Praeger).

Kaloupek DG, Scott JR, Khatami V. Assessment of coping strategies associated with syncope in blood donors. J Psychosom Res. 1985;29:207-214.

Kanwisher, N. (2001) Neural events and perceptual awareness. Cognition 79, 89-113; also reprinted inS. Dehaene (ed.) The Cognitive Neuroscience of Consciousness. Cambridge, MA, MIT Press, 89-113.

Kapleau, Roshi P. (1980) The Three Pillars of Zen: Teaching, Practice, and Enlightenment (revised edn). New York, Doubleday.

Karn, K. and Hayhoe, M. (2000) Memory representations guide targeting eye movements in a natural task. Visual Cognition 7, 673-703.

Kasamatsu, A. and Hirai, T. (1966) An electroencephalographic study on the Zen meditation (zazen). Folia Psychiatrica et Neurologica Japonica 20, 315-36.

Kaiserman-Abramof, I. R., Graybiel, A. M., & Nauta, W. J. (1980). The thalamic projection to cortical area 17 in a congenitally anophthalmic mouse strain. Neuroscience, 5, 41–52.

Kanold, P. O., Kara, P., Reid, R. C., & Shatz, C. J. (2003). Role of subplate neurons in functional maturation of visual cortical columns. Science, 301, 521–525.

Kennedy, H., & Dehay, C. (1988). Functional implications of the anatomical organization of the callosal projections of visual areas V1 and V2 in the macaque monkey. Behav. Brain Res., 29, 225–236.

Kentridge, R.W. and Heywood, C.A. (1999) The status of blindsight. Journal of Consciousness Studies 6(5), 3-11.

Kihlstrom, J.F. (1996) Perception without awareness of what is perceived, learning without awareness of what is learned. In M. Velmans (ed.) The Science of Consciousness. London, Routledge, 23-46.

Kollerstrom, N. (1999) The path of Halley's comet, and Newton's late apprehension of the law of gravity. Annals of Science 56, 331-56.

Kosslyn, S.M. (1980) Image and Mind. Cambridge, MA, Harvard University Press.

Kosslyn, S.M. (1988) Aspects of a cognitive neuroscience of mental imagery. Science 240, 1621-6.

Kinsbourne, M. (1995), 'The intralaminar thalamic nucleii', Consciousness and Cognition, 4.

Kjaer, Troels, Camilla Bertelsen, Paola Piccini, David Brooks, Jorgen Alving, and Hans Lou. "Increased Dopamine Tone during Meditation- Induced Change of Consciousness." Cognitive Brain Research 13, no. 2 (April 2002)

Kölmel HW. 1985. Complex visual hallucinations in the hemianopic field. J Neurol Neurosurg Psychiatry.

Koenig, Harold. "Research on Religion, Spirituality, and Mental Health: A Review." Canadian Journal of Psychiatry 54, no. 5 (May 2009)

Koenig, Harold, ed. Handbook of Religion and Mental Health. San Diego, CA: Academic Press, 1998

Kraepelin E. Psychiatry: A Textbook for Students and Physicians. New York, NY: Science History Publications; 1990.

Lauglin, Charles, John McManus, and Eugene d'Aquili. Brain, Symbol, and Experience. 2nd ed. New York: Columbia University Press, 1992

Lakoff, G. and M. Johnson (1999). Philosophy in the flesh. Basic Books: New York.

LeDoux, J. E. (1996). The emotional brain. New York: Simon & Schuster.

LeDoux, J.E. (1992), 'Emotion and the amygdala', in The Amygdala:

Neurobiological Aspects of Emo- tion, Memory and Mental Dysfunction, ed J.P. Aggleton (New York: Wiley-Liss).

Levin, D.T. and Simons, D.J. (1997) Failure to detect changes to attended objects in motion pictures. Psychonomic Bulletin and Review 4, 501-6.

Levine,J. (1983) Materialism and qualia: the explanatory gap. Pacific Philosophical Quarterly 64, 354-61.

Levine,J. (2001) Purple Haze: The Puzzle of Consciousness. New York, Oxford University Press. Levine, S. (1979) A Gradual Awakening. New York, Doubleday.

Levinson, B.W. (1965) States of awareness during general anaesthesia. British Journal of Anaesthesia 37, 544-6.

Lewicki, P., Czyzewska, M. and Hoffman, H. (1987) Unconscious acquisition of complex procedural knowledge. Journal of Experimental Psychology: Learning, Memory and Cognition 13, 523-30.

Lewicki, P., Hill, T. and Bizot, E. (1988) Acquisition of procedural knowledge about a pattern of stimuli that cannot be articulated. Cognitive Psychology 20, 24-37.

Lewicki, P., Hill, T. and Czyzewska, M. (1992) Nonconscious acquisition of information. American Psychologist 47, 796-801.

Manthey S, Schubotz RI, von Cramon DY (2003). Premotor cortex in observing erroneous action: an fMRI study. Brain Res Cogn Brain Res 15: 296–307.

Mesulam MM, Mufson EJ (1982) Insula of the old world monkey. III: Efferent cortical output and comments on function. J Comp Neurol 212: 38–52.

Naskar, Abhijit. "Homo: A Brief History of Consciousness", 2015

Naskar, Abhijit. "What is Mind?", 2016

Naskar, Abhijit. "Love, God & Neurons: Memoir of A Scientist who found himself by getting lost", 2016

Naskar, Abhijit. "Principia Humanitas", 2017

Naskar, Abhijit. "We Are All Black: A Treatise on Racism", 2017

Naskar, Abhijit. "Either Civilized or Phobic: A Treatise on Homosexuality", 2017

Naskar, Abhijit. "I Am The Thread: My Mission", 2017

Naskar, Abhijit. "The Bengal Tigress: A Treatise on Gender Equality", 2017

Naskar, Abhijit. "Morality Absolute", 2017

Naskar, Abhijit. "Build Bridges not Walls: In the name of Americana", 2018

Naskar, Abhijit. "Fabric of Humanity", 2018

Naskar, Abhijit. "Lives To Serve Before I Sleep", 2019

Naskar, Abhijit. "Citizens of Peace: Beyond the Savagery of Sovereignty", 2019

Naskar, Abhijit. "The Constitution of The United Peoples of Earth", 2019

Naskar, Abhijit. "Neurons Giveth, Neurons Taketh Away | Abhijit Naskar | TEDxIIMRanchi", 2019 https://www.youtube.com/watch?v=BNX-Q0ySm80

Naskar, Abhijit. "Mission Reality", 2019

Naskar, Abhijit. "Operation Justice: To Make A Society That Needs No Law", 2019

Naskar, Abhijit. "Every Generation Needs Caretakers: The Gospel of Patriotism", 2020

Naskar, Abhijit. "Revolution Indomable", 2020

Naskar, Abhijit. "Servitude is Sanctitude", 2020

Naskar, Abhijit. "Time To End Democracy: The Meritocratic Manifesto", 2020

Newberg, Andrew, and Jeremy Iversen. "The Neural Basis of the Complex Mental Task of Meditation: Neurotransmitter and Neurochemical Considerations." Medical Hypotheses 61, no. 2 (2003).

Newberg, Andrew. "How God Changes Your Brain: An Introduction to Jewish Neurotheology", CCAR Journal: The Reform Jewish Quarterly, Winter 2016.

Newberg, Andrew, and Stephanie Newberg. "A Neuropsychological Perspective on Spiritual Development." In Handbook of Spiritual Development in Childhood and Adolescence, edited by Eugene Roehlkepartain, Pamela King, Linda Wagener, and Peter Benson. London: Sage Publications, Inc., 2005

Newberg, Andrew. "The Neurotheology Link An Intersection Between Spirituality and Health", Alternative and Complimentary Therapies, Vol 21 No 1, February 2015.

Newberg, Andrew, Nancy Wintering, Dharma Khalsa, Hannah Roggenkamp, and Mark Waldman. "Meditation Effects on Cognitive Function and Cerebral Blood Flow in Subjects with Memory Loss: A Preliminary Study." Journal of Alzheimer's Disease 20, no. 2 (2010)

Nash, M. (1995), 'Glimpses of the mind', Time.

Nesse RM. Proximate and evolutionary studies of anxiety, stress and depression: synergy at the interface. Neurosci Biobehav Rev. 1999;23:895-903.

Nicolelis, Miguel. (2011) "Beyond Boundaries: The New Neuroscience of Connecting Brains with Machines--- and How It Will Change Our Lives", Times Books

O'Hara, K. and Scutt, T. (1996) There is no hard problem of consciousness. Journal of Consciousness Studies 3(4), 290-302, reprinted in J. Shear (ed.) (1997) Explaining Consciousness. Cambridge, MA, MIT Press, 69-82.

O'Regan, J.K. (1992) Solving the "real" mysteries of visual perception: the world as an outside memory. Canadian Journal of Psychology 46, 461-88.

O'Regan, J.K. and Noe, A. (2001) A sensorimotor account of vision and visual consciousness. Behavioral and Brain Sciences 24(5), 883-917.

O'Regan, J.K., Rensink, R.A. and Clark,].]. (1999) Change-blindness as a result of "mudsplashes." Nature 398, 34.

Ornstein, R.E. (1977) The Psychology of Consciousness (2nd edn). New York, Harcourt.

Ornstein, R.E. (1986) The Psychology of Consciousness (3rd edn). New York, Pehguin.

Ornstein, R.E. (1992) The Evolution of Consciousness. New York, Touchstone.

Penfield W, Faulk ME (1955) The insula: further observations on its function. Brain 78: 445– 470.

Penrose, R. (1994), Shadows of the Mind (Oxford: Oxford University Press).

Penrose, R. (1989), The Emperor's New Mind: Concerning Computers, Minds and The Laws of Physics (Oxford: Oxford University Press).

Persinger, "'I would kill in God's name' role of sex, weekly church attendance, report of a religious experience and limbic lability" Perceptual and Motor Skills 1997.

Persinger "Experimental simulation of the God experience" Neurotheology 2003.

Persinger, M. A. (1993b). Personality changes following brain injury as a grief response to the loss of sense of self: Phenomenological themes as indices of local lability and neurocognitive restructuring as psycho- therapy. Psychological Reports, 72

Persinger, Corradini, Clement, Keaney, et al "Neurotheology and its convergence with neuroquantology" NeuroQuantology 2010.

Persinger, Koren and St-Pierre "The electromagnetic induction of mystical and altered states within the laboratory" Journal of Consciousness Exploration and Research 2010.

Persinger "Case report: A prototypical spontaneous 'sensed presence' of a sentient being and concomitant electroencephalographic activity in the clinical laboratory" Neurocase 2008.

Persinger and Saroka "Potential production of Hughlings Jackson's "parasitic consciousness" by physiologically-patterned weak transcerebral magnetic fields: QEEG and source localization" Epilepsy & Behavior 28 (2013).

Persinger. "The neuropsychiatry of paranormal experiences". J Neuropsychiatry Clin Neurosci 2001.

Persinger. "Neuropsychological bases of god beliefs", New York: Praeger, 1987

Persinger. "Temporal lobe epileptic signs and correlative behaviors displayed by normal populations", Journal of General Psychology, 1986

Perry BD, Pollard R. Homeostasis, stress, trauma, and adaptation. A neurodevelopmental view of childhood trauma. Child Adolesc Psychiatr Clin N Am. 1998;7:33.

Paré, D. & Llinás, R. (1995), 'Conscious and preconscious processes as seen from the standpoint of sleep-waking cycle neurophysiology', Neuropsychologia, 33.

P. S. de Laplace. Essai Philosophique sur les Probabilites [1814], in Academy des Sciences, Oeuvres Complotes de Laplace, Vol. 7, Gauthier-Villars, Paris (1886).

Perrett DI, Harries MH, Bevan R, Thomas S, Benson PJ, Mistlin AJ, Chitty AJ, Hietanen JK, Ortega JE (1989) Frameworks of analysis for the neural representation of animate objects and actions. J Exp Bio 146: 87–113.

Phillips ML, Young AW, Senior C, Brammer M, Andrew C, Calder AJ, Bullmore ET, Perrett DI, Rowland D, Williams SC, Gray JA, David AS (1997) A specific neural substrate for perceiving facial expressions of disgust. Nature 389: 495–498.

Phillips ML, Young AW, Scott SK, Calder AJ, Andrew C, Giampietro V, Williams SC, Bullmore ET, Brammer M, Gray JA (1998) Neural responses to facial and vocal expressions of fear and disgust. Proc R Soc Lond B Biol Sci 265: 1809–1817.

Puce A, Perrett D (2003) Electrophysiological and brain imaging of biological motion. Philosoph Trans Royal Soc Lond, Series B, 358: 435–445.

Ramachandran VS. Behavioral and magnetoencephalographic correlates of plasticity in the adult human brain. Proc Natl Acad Sci USA 1993; 90: 10413–20.

Ramachandran VS. Phantom limbs, neglect syndromes, repressed memories, and Freudian psychology. Int Rev Neurobiol 1994; 37: 291–333.

Ramachandran VS. Plasticity and functional recovery in neurology. Clin Med 2005; 5: 368–73.

Ramachandran VS, Hirstein W. The perception of phantom limbs. The D. O. Hebb lecture. Brain 1998; 121: 1603–30.

Ramachandran VS, Rogers-Ramachandran D, Cobb S. Touching the phantom limb. Nature 1995; 377: 489–90.

Ramachandran VS, Rogers-Ramachandran D. Phantom limbs and

neural plasticity. Arch Neurol 2000; 57: 317–20.

Ramachandran VS, Rogers-Ramachandran D. It's all done with mirrors. Sci Am Mind 2007; 18: 16–9.

Ramachandran VS, Rogers-Ramachandran D. Sensations referred to a patient's phantom arm from another subjects intact arm: perceptual correlates of mirror neurons. Med Hypotheses 2008; 70: 1233–4.

Ramachandran VS, Rogers-Ramachandran D, Stewart M. Perceptual correlates of massive cortical reorganization. Science 1992; 258: 1159–60.

Rizzolatti G, Craighero L (2004) The mirror-neuron system. Annu Rev Neurosci 27: 169–192.

Rizzolatti G, Fogassi L, Gallese V (2001) Neurophysiological mechanisms underlying the understanding and imitation of action. Nature Rev Neurosci 2:661–670.

Rock I, Victor J. Vision and touch: an experimentally created conflict between the two senses. Science 1964; 143: 594–6.

Rose´n B, Lundborg G. Training with a mirror in rehabilitation of the hand. Scand J Plast Reconstr Surg Hand Surg 2005; 39: 104–8.

Royet JP, Plailly J, Delon-Martin C, Kareken DA, Segebarth C (2003) fMRI of emotional responses to odors: influence of hedonic valence and judgment, handedness, and gender. Neuroimage 20: 713–728.

Rozin R Haidt J and McCauley CR (2000) Disgust. In: Lewis M, Haviland-Jones JM (eds) Handbook of Emotion. 2nd Edition. Guilford Press, New York, pp 637–653.

Saxe R, Carey S, Kanwisher N (2004) Understanding other minds: linking developmental psychology and functional neuroimaging. Annu Rev Psychol 55: 87–124.

S. J. Russell and P. Norvig, Artificial intelligence: a modern approach (3rd edition): Prentice Hall, 2009.

Schienle A, Stark R, Walter B, Blecker C, Ott U, Kirsch P, Sammer G, Vaitl D (2002) The insula is not specifically involved in disgust processing: an fMRI study. Neuroreport 13: 2023–2026.

Showers MJC, Lauer EW (1961) Somatovisceral motor patterns in the insula. J Comp Neurol 117: 107–115.

Singer T, Seymour B, O'Doherty J, Kaube H, Dolan RJ, Frith CD (2004) Empathy for pain involves the affective but not the sensory components of pain. Science 303: 1157–1162.

Smith A (1759) The theory of moral sentiments (ed. 1976). Clarendon Press, Oxford.

S. N. Bose (1924). "Plancks Gesetz und Lichtquantenhypothese". Zeitschrift für Physik. 26 (1): 178–181.

Sprengelmeyer R, Rausch M, Eysel UT, Przuntek H (1998) Neural structures associated with recognition of facial expressions of basic emotions Proc R Soc Lond B Biol Sci 265: 1927–1931.

Strafella AP, Paus T (2000) Modulation of cortical excitability during action observation: a transcranial magnetic stimulation study. NeuroReport 11: 2289–2292.

Simonsen R (2015) Eating for the future: veganism and the challenge of in vitro meat. In: Stapleton P, Byers A (Hg). Biopolitics and utopia. Palgrave Macmillan, New York (2015), S 167–190

Tanaka K (1996) Inferotemporal cortex and object vision. Ann Rev Neurosci. 19: 109–140.

Tesla N. "My Inventions", 1919

T. R. Society, "Machine learning: the power and promise of computers that learn by example," ed. The Royal Society, 2017.

Tomasello M, Call J (1997) Primate cognition. Oxford University Press, Oxford.

Tremblay C, Robert M, Pascual-Leone A, Lepore F, Nguyen DK, Carmant L, Bouthillier A, Theoret H (2004) Action observation and execution: intracranial recordings in a human subject. Neurology. 63: 937–938.

Umilta MA, Kohler E, Gallese V, Fogassi L, Fadiga L, Keysers C, Rizzolatti G (2001) "I know what you are doing": a neurophysiological study. Neuron 32: 91–101.

Von Wright G.H., (1963), Norm and Action. A Logical Inquiry, Routledge & Kegan Paul, London.

Von Wright G.H., (1976), "Determinism and the Study of Man", in Essays on Explanation and Understanding, ed. by J. Manninen and R. Tuomela, Reidel, Dordrecht.

Von Wright G.H., (1977), "What is Humanism?", The Lindlay Lecture, University of Arkansas, Lawrence, Kansas.

Von Wright G.H., (1979), "Humanism and the Humanities", in Philosophy and Grammar, ed. by S. Kanger and S. Öhman, Reidel, Dordrecht, pp. 1-16. Reprinted in von Wright (1993).

Von Wright G.H., (1980), Freedom and Determination, North-Holland Publishing Co., Amsterdam.

Von Wright G.H., (1985), Of Human Freedom, The Tanner Lectures on Human Values,

Vol. VI, ed. by S. M. McMurrin, University of Utah Press, Salt Lake City, pp. 107-70. Reprinted in von Wright (1998).

Von Wright G.H., (1993), The Tree of Knowledge and Other Essays, Brill, Leiden.

Von Wright G.H., (1997), "Progress: Fact and Fiction", in The Idea of Progress, ed. by A. Burgen et al., W. de Gruyter, Berlin, pp. 1-18.

Von Wright G.H., (1998), In the Shadow of Descartes: Essays in the Philosophy of Mind, Kluwer, Dordrecht.